MW01131333

PYTHONS

BY LIBBY WILSON

Copyright © 2024 by Apex Editions, Mendota Heights, MN 55120. All rights reserved. No part of this book may be reproduced or utilized in any form or by any means without written permission from the publisher.

Apex is distributed by North Star Editions:
sales@northstareditions.com | 888-417-0195

Produced for Apex by Red Line Editorial.

Photographs ©: Shutterstock Images, cover, 1, 4–5, 6, 7, 8–9, 10–11, 12, 13, 14–15, 16–17, 18, 20, 21, 22–23, 24–25, 27, 29

Library of Congress Control Number: 2023910144

ISBN
978-1-63738-775-7 (hardcover)
978-1-63738-818-1 (paperback)
978-1-63738-899-0 (ebook pdf)
978-1-63738-861-7 (hosted ebook)

Printed in the United States of America
Mankato, MN
012024

NOTE TO PARENTS AND EDUCATORS

Apex books are designed to build literacy skills in striving readers. Exciting, high-interest content attracts and holds readers' attention. The text is carefully leveled to allow students to achieve success quickly. Additional features, such as bolded glossary words for difficult terms, help build comprehension.

TABLE OF CONTENTS

CHAPTER 1

SURPRISE ATTACK

A python hides in the grass by a river. The snake lies still and waits for **prey** to come near.

Pythons usually don't chase their prey. Instead, they hide and surprise prey.

The python flicks out its tongue to smell the air. It notices a deer nearby. When the deer bends down to drink, the python strikes.

A python's tongue is forked. This shape helps the snake pick up and follow smells.

Pythons often wait near water to catch prey.

SENSING SMELLS

A python flicks its tongue to collect smells. The tongue touches an **organ** in the snake's mouth. This organ helps the snake's brain tell what the smell is.

The snake curls around the deer. The deer can't move or escape. The python's grip gets tighter and tighter. Soon, the deer dies. The snake swallows it whole.

FAST FACT

Pythons can go months without eating.

A python squeezes until its prey's heart stops beating.

CHAPTER 2

TYPES OF PYTHONS

There are many different kinds of pythons. Some can grow 33 feet (10 m) long. Others are less than 2 feet (0.6 m) long.

Reticulated pythons often grow more than 20.5 feet (6.25 m) long. They are the world's longest snakes.

Indian pythons live in forests in South Asia.

Pythons are **native** to Africa, Asia, and Australia. They make their homes in a variety of warm **habitats**. These include forests, grasslands, and swamps.

WATER LOVERS

Pythons often live near water. Some types such as Burmese pythons are excellent swimmers. They can stay underwater for 30 minutes. And they are sometimes found miles out into the ocean.

Pythons usually swim in freshwater rivers or lakes.

Woma pythons live in dry areas in Australia. They blend in with dirt or sand.

A python's scales can be many colors. Often, these colors match the snake's habitat. This helps the snake hide from prey or danger.

FAST FACT

Womas are some of the only pythons that dig their own burrows.

CHAPTER 3

CATCHING PREY

Pythons are fierce **predators**. Small pythons eat animals like lizards and mice. Larger pythons can catch bigger prey. They may eat deer, pigs, or monkeys.

Some pythons eat rodents such as mice, rats, and gerbils.

Most pythons have **pits** on their faces. The pits sense body heat from nearby animals. That helps pythons find prey.

FAST FACT

Some pythons can hunt alligators. Alligators have few other predators.

A python's pits look like a row of holes near its mouth.

Pythons are **constrictors**. They bite to catch prey. But they squeeze to kill it. A python's tight grip makes it hard for prey to breathe. It also stops the prey's blood from flowing.

A python squeezes tighter each time its prey breathes out.

A python's skin is stretchy. Its body bulges after a big meal.

SWALLOWING

A python can swallow an animal six times its size. The python's jaws stretch very wide. Rows of teeth help, too. These teeth point backward. They pull prey into the python's mouth.

CHAPTER 4

LIFE CYCLE

Pythons usually live alone. But they come together to **mate**. After mating, females lay eggs.

A female python can lay up to 100 eggs at a time.

Females wrap around their eggs to keep them warm. The eggs take a few months to hatch. In the meantime, the mothers don't eat. They may lose about half their weight.

Babies stay with their mothers for two weeks after hatching.

HEAT CHECK

Female pythons check their eggs' temperature. Their pits sense tiny changes in heat. If the eggs are cold, the pythons shiver. This makes more heat.

After hatching, young pythons face danger. Animals such as birds and wild dogs might eat them. But the snakes soon grow into top predators.

FAST FACT

In the wild, many pythons live for around 15 years.

Pythons sometimes climb trees to hide or hunt. ▶

COMPREHENSION QUESTIONS

Write your answers on a separate piece of paper.

1. Write a sentence describing one place pythons live.

2. What fact about pythons is most interesting to you? Why?

3. How does a python kill its prey?

    A. by biting

    B. by squeezing

    C. with poison

4. Why might young pythons face more danger than adult pythons?

    A. The young snakes have no scales.

    B. The young snakes are heavier.

    C. The young snakes are smaller.

5. What does **variety** mean in this book?

*They make their homes in a **variety** of warm habitats. These include forests, grasslands, and swamps.*

    A. a few different types
    B. the exact same type
    C. very small types

6. What does **temperature** mean in this book?

*Female pythons check their eggs' **temperature.** Their pits sense tiny changes in heat.*

    A. how hard or soft something is
    B. how hot or cold something is
    C. how big or small something is

Answer key on page 32.

GLOSSARY

constrictors
Snakes that kill by wrapping their bodies around prey and squeezing.

habitats
The places where animals normally live.

mate
To come together to have babies.

native
Originally living in an area.

organ
A part of the body that has a specific job.

pits
Holes on the faces of some snakes that are used to sense heat.

predators
Animals that hunt and eat other animals.

prey
Animals that are hunted and eaten by other animals.

BOOKS

Klepeis, Alicia Z. *Burmese Pythons*. Minneapolis: Jump!, 2023.

Murray, Julie. *Pythons*. Minneapolis: Abdo Publishing, 2020.

Terp, Gail. *Pythons*. Mankato, MN: Black Rabbit Books, 2021.

ONLINE RESOURCES

Visit **www.apexeditions.com** to find links and resources related to this title.

ABOUT THE AUTHOR

Libby Wilson is a retired elementary librarian. She loves to research and share amazing facts about nature with readers. Ms. Wilson would like to thank the Conservancy of Southwest Florida for their important work and for answering her question about pythons.

INDEX

ANSWER KEY:
1. Answers will vary; 2. Answers will vary; 3. B; 4. C; 5. A; 6. B